T0072418

Seven Steps to
FREEDOM

DARRELL MOWAT

WESTBOW°
PRESS
A DIVISION OF THOMAS NELSON
& ZONDERVAN

WestBow Press books may be ordered through booksellers or by contacting:

WestBow Press
A Division of Thomas Nelson & Zondervan
1663 Liberty Drive
Bloomington, IN 47403
www.westbowpress.com
1 (866) 928-1240

ISBN: 978-1-4908-3321-7 (sc)
ISBN: 978-1-4908-3322-4 (e)

Library of Congress Control Number: 2014906609

Printed in the United States of America.

WestBow Press rev. date: 08/07/2014

Contents

Acknowledgements

To everyone who made this Bible study possible thank you and to God be the glory!

Seven Steps to Freedom is dedicated to everyone who is in captivity right now. Keep up the good fight. There is a light at the end of the tunnel.

Before starting this study keep an open mind and if you have a higher power ask for wisdom and understanding for this book to enter your heart.

Introduction

I never thought I would see the inside of a jail cell. As a child I always thought if I started smoking I would get involved with a gang and start stealing, so I did my best to stay away from that stuff.

But God has a funny way of working out a person's preconceived notions of others, even as a child. As He says, "Judge not, and you will not be judged" (Luke 6:37). So after eight years of a relatively blissful life as a child my mother and father had a divorce. With my life situation abruptly changed it was now time for the next phase of my life.

It was not always easy growing up in a single parent home. Thank God my mom and dad did the best they could when I was young to prepare me for life. My dad taught me the basics in using tools and encouraged scouting activities as a young child. And my mom took me to community activities for reading, sports and play time with other children.

As I grew older I started swaying from my upbringing. I hung-out with neighbourhood friends and school mates where, at times, we caused some minor trouble and mischief. I was bullied and abused by some of these people and I had done the same to others. But in the end we did enjoy ourselves, as well, learning how to play our schoolyard games and get along in the world.

As I moved on and high school was right around the corner, I was entering a new world of responsibility. College or work was just five years away and either one required focus in order to succeed. Again, unfortunately I chose a more reckless path for a time. I enjoyed high school life, as I had a good educational foundation from elementary school. I started working part-time on the weekends during school and fulltime during the summer. With the money, instead of saving it for college, I drank it away on the weekends, bought a car and invested in loud car stereo equipment.

I thought this was all grand until my drinking got out of control and I lost my vehicle and almost lost my life.

After this wakeup call, I decided it was time to "pull up my socks" and do the right thing. This meant focusing on a University career path.

University was a culture-shock at first, big buildings, more students and an incredible infrastructure, not to mention the diversity of nationalities of the student and faculty groups. It was a great and refreshing change in my life and I embraced it.

I can remember the first class I sat in. I said to myself "Wow, I cannot believe I am here". Being in awe for a few minutes, I finally realized, "Well I better start listening and studying or I will not be here for very long". So that was the start of my University career.

It took four years to complete the studies required to meet my degree choice. And I enjoyed every minute of it. I met new people, learned new things about myself, the world and had the chance to travel while doing it. Namely, I was part of a team that designed, constructed, and raced a canoe of concrete. This was the start of learning how to lead a group of people to a common goal.

In my final year of University I realized I had some decisions to make. I had a small fortune in debt and the desire to accomplish more. I was not ready for the "working world" and I found an option of joining the military would be an opportune choice at the time. This worked because they had a signing bonus for engineers, which was my discipline and the possibility to become a pilot, as I had dreamed about being one over the years past.

With that path as a good option and graduation right around the corner, I "got serious" and started the application process. During this time before I joined there were a few bumps in the road. That is, my Grandfather passed away and my mother had cancer, but nevertheless it was time to move onto the next chapter of my life.

In advance of starting my military training I took one last look at the world and went on a three week trip to Europe. It was beautiful and I became a little more in touch with my ancestral roots. It was also good testing grounds for preparing to march with heavy equipment on one's back, as I backpacked for most of the trip.

When I arrived back home I worked for a bit and then that winter it was off to basic training. During those 2 and one half years in the military I learned a lot about leadership and how to follow as well. It has prepared me mentally and physically for many trials in my life. I met many wonderful people just like in University and it helped prepare me for the next step on my life's journey.

After two years of training I finally realized that the military was not for me at least at that point in my life. Many issues were gnawing at me from back home and I could no longer focus properly to serve the way I was expected to. So I asked for a voluntary release...

Although it took 6 months, the paper work went through and I was on my way home. During this period I had time to reflect on my past and what I had done with my life. I was also being reintroduced to God, who I learned about as a child. And I could see that my life was heading down yet another path. After being released from the military I spent some time in the city I was living in at the time, looking for work, but ultimately headed back to where I was born.

The next few years were a whirlwind of events that would eventually lead me into a place I had never expected to be. I found a job in my field of work after some searching and a small spiritual break after leaving the military and finally settled in an apartment in my home town. However that did not last long and I was on my way again. Soon after being laid off, I moved back in with my mother and was working part-time in the financial industry. Little did I know my life was about to change for the better, but not before one last major detour.

I started volunteering on a farm around the same time and it was working out well, but one of the choices I made while working there landed me, eventually, behind bars. This brings us almost to the point of this study. "…all things God works for the good of those who love him…" (Romans 8:28).

The time in prison although not lengthy (6 months) compared to my entire life was significant in that I had time to reflect and reassess what direction I was travelling in. I also had time to make some concrete plans to head in the right direction, once I was released, which led to the book you are currently reading, amongst other great plans.

Although all life decisions do not always lead to an immediate "happy ever after ending", it is my hope that your decision to pick up this book is a part of yours. As I know it was a joy to write it!

Enjoy and take time to really understand your purpose here on earth.

STEP 1: Accepting God's Love

"Greater love has no one than this:
to lay down one's life for one's friends."
—JOHN 15:13

Story: Common Ground

A young man, whose life experience was going down a different road than most of his immediate family's had, had some choices to make. After years of just "getting by" in high school, he finally realized, with some help, that he needed to change his attitude and thought process if he was ever going to succeed in University.

After a year of readjusting and regaining some of the confidence of his childhood, he recognized that it was very possible to succeed and graduate where none of his family had before him. Above all he met a friend, a teacher's aide, who would teach him things about himself and the world he never thought possible. This friend was not the same skin colour or even from the same side of the world as the student, but the bond and friendship they developed was unparalleled in this young man's life before that.

This experience goes to show you that God can work through anybody. They do not have to be the same skin colour, come from the same country or even be in the same "religion" as you are, but the bonds that are developed are very much the one's God creates between loving, caring human beings. Sometimes these bonds last a life time or only for a fleeting moment but the memories last forever.

In the epistle to the Romans it is mentioned "Indeed, when Gentiles, who do not have the law, do by nature things required by the law, they are a law for themselves, even though they do not have the law. They show that the requirements of the law are written on their hearts, their consciences also bearing witness, and their thoughts sometimes accusing them and at other times even defending them." (Romans 2:14–15)

When reading through this lesson think about the common ground one shares with other human beings from different races and religions so you can start building friendships on that truth.

Lesson: Sacrifice

Golden Rule: Do unto others as you would have done unto yourself. Every major world religion has this rule in common and a God they should love.

In Christianity all of God's laws can be wrapped up in two commandments. "Love the Lord your God with all your heart and with all your soul and with all your mind... and... Love your neighbor as yourself" (Matthew 22:37–40).

Jesus goes one further during His ministry and says "...love your enemies and pray for those who persecute you, that you may be children of your Father in heaven." (Matthew 5:44, 45). Jesus showed all of God's love to us through His ministry:

- He preached the coming kingdom of heaven (Mark 1:15, Matthew 4:17, Luke 10:9).

- He laid His life down on the cross for us as a sinless man to take all of our sins on His life (Luke 23:33, 2 Corinthians 5:21).

- God resurrected His body after three days in a tomb so that Jesus is now alive in heaven awaiting His return to earth (Matthew 17:23).

- And to all those who believe; He gave His Holy Spirit to dwell in us until He comes with all His glory (2 Timothy 1:14, Ephesians 1:13, 14).

Jesus was tempted before His ministry began (Matthew 4:1–11). He faced trials during His ministry (Luke 22:28). And He defeated the enemy through His death and resurrection. Jesus did all of this to fulfill God's plan to save us from our sins and give us the opportunity to have the gift of eternal life in His kingdom (John 3:16).

NOTES

_____

_____

_____

_____

Discussion: Knowledge

"Where there is love there is life"
—MAHATMA GHANDI

Christ laid his life down for us in order to stand for the truth! When reading and answering questions to this step's discussion, focus on the simple things Christ did for us.

Discussion Questions

1. How do you relate your personal belief system with other religions, people and belief systems?

   _____

   _____

   _____

   _____

   _____

2. Do you look for common ground with yourself and others or do you separate yourself from others based on differences?

   _____

   _____

   _____

   _____

   _____

3. How can a person reconcile ones' belief system with other religions, people and belief systems? List some ideas.

_____

_____

_____

_____

_____

4. How do you relate your faith journey with respect to the roots of Christianity? That is, the people (Jesus, Paul, Peter, etc.) previously of the Jewish faith whom it was founded by. Read John 4:22 and Romans 3:1, 2 for some insight.

_____

_____

_____

_____

_____

5. Pick out at least one place in the Bible (New Testament) that suggests Jesus was a practicing Jew.

_____

_____

_____

_____

_____

STEP 2: What Should We Do?

"Yet to all who did receive him, to those who believed in his name, he gave the right to become children of God."

—JOHN 1:12

Story: Decisions

A young man who had just finished University joined the military. He had always admired leadership in his country and wanted to do his part to serve the country that had protected his right to freedom since he was a young child.

Little did he know that God had a different plan. He joined, but a couple of years in he saw that, although the forces were a great career path and a wonderful life experience, it was not for him.

After six months of mulling over options with military career staff, he finally decided to leave. Hoping and trusting in the Lord to lead him for the remainder of his life.

At times in life you are left with choices. They are not always easy, but they have to be made. If God is speaking to you, even using these pages, you probably have choices to make. Take time and "mull" over the decision(s) that might have to be made. As the Bible says, "…hasty feet miss the way." (Proverbs 19:2).

Take time, read through this lesson and ask God what He has in store for you. Make clear the decisions that appear before you!

Lesson: Acceptance

Accept God into your life. No person can make you do this; it has to be a personal decision. Accept that you are a sinner and that you do not have control over your own life (Matthew 19:17).

There are two forces at work in this world, good and evil and every day we make our choice as to which side we are going to be on, the good or the bad (Matthew 7:15–20).

If it were up to God, He would have us choose His way every day, but because He loves us so much He gave us the option to choose; His way or the way of the world (John 1:13).

Unfortunately, left to our own decisions we often choose the wrong way which separates us from Him (Mark 7:20–23). However, God never wants us to take that path (Deuteronomy 20:19).

Thank God, He knew that left to our own devices we would turn from Him. That is why He sent His only Son down to earth to be the atonement for our sins. Now all we have to do is accept Him into our life (John 10:7–17).

Praise God that Jesus, His Son, died for our sins and was raised back up to heaven, having defeated Satan and his multitudes. Do you realize this? If so you have an option. You can continue your life as you are or you can accept the blood of Jesus in your life to wash away your sins. Turn to God in earnest prayer asking Him for forgiveness, through Christ, for everything you have ever done against Him. This is called repentance (Matthew 3:2).

God is more than ready to accept your prayers for forgiveness. Jesus spoke of the lost sheep that ran away from the flock. The shepherd left the ninety-nine to save the one who was lost. This is how He feels about us (Luke 15:4–7).

NOTES

_____

_____

_____

_____

_____

_____

_____

_____

_____

_____

_____

_____

_____

_____

_____

_____

Discussion: Planning

"The destiny of man is not measured by material computation, when great forces are on the move in the world, we learn we are spirits, not animals."
—Sir Winston Churchill

Soldiers of our nations are expected to make the ultimate sacrifice for their country and fellow man when asked to. Never are they asked to blindly lose their lives. They are part of a calculated and accurately made "bigger plan". When reading and answering questions to this step's discussion keep in mind what purpose God has for you in His "bigger plan".

Discussion Questions

1. What choices do you have to make in your life currently? List them out and make clear the options you could take for each of them.

_____

_____

_____

_____

_____

2. If it came down to it would you be ready to make the ultimate sacrifice for your beliefs? Why or why not?

_____

_____

_____

_____

3. What changes could you make in your daily routine that would have a positive impact on you and the world around you?

_____

_____

_____

_____

_____

4. What choices have you made in the past that have changed your life, positive or negative? List them out.

_____

_____

_____

_____

_____

5. If negative, what can you do to use those negative choices and turn them into positives for yourself and others who can learn from them?

_____

_____

_____

_____

_____

STEP 3: The Right Path

"Enter through the narrow gate. For wide is the gate and broad is the road that leads to destruction, and many enter through it."
—MATTHEW 7:13

Story: Revelation

A young man who had recently learned about Jesus and the knowledge of a life after earth was stuck at a cross roads in life; he could continue down the path to destruction or try this "new idea" called following Jesus.

Little did he know that he still had a few hard lessons to learn before he would completely submit his will to God. After attending some churches and embracing his new found faith he was sent away from fellowship. Disillusioned and upset he stopped praying and reading the Bible and hoped that God alone would lead him in the correct direction.

The result was a mound of debt and then jail, both of which he had never considered, never mind experienced before in his life.

Even with these unexpected hardships he decided to "pull up his socks" and take responsibility as he always had. He chose to pick up the Bible and start reading again. This decision would change the rest of his life and for the better!

Occasionally in life we hit road blocks, especially as new believers. But we must ask ourselves, "Why is this all happening?" instead of playing the blame game. Keeping a daily routine of right decisions is important and this is the beginning of the right path. While reading through this lesson, consider the revelation that is taking place and how this fits in with your plans for the future?

Lesson: Plans

What is the right path you might ask? It is a personal and loving relationship with God, through His only begotten Son, Jesus Christ (Matthew 11:28–30). At first this path may not seem easy, as it is a "narrow gate", but those who choose to "enter through" are destined for blessings and love in this life and much more in the life to come (Luke 12:37).

The right path is no longer your path. It is the path chosen by God for you. You must choose to die to your old self, your old ways, and your old habits. By doing this you are cleansed and set apart to develop new ways and new habits (2 Corinthians 5:14–17, James 1:21). This new life of yours must be directed by God, through your prayers and praise, reading God's Word and fellowshipping with other believers (Ephesians 4:21–24, Acts 6:4).

We need to pray and give praise to God in order to keep in contact with Him and show Him our gratitude for all He has done for us (Luke 19:37, 38). You might say what has He done for me, lately? Just look around and see, the trees, the birds, shelter, family and friends, food, all created by the hands of God. Right communication with others is the key to growth on earth, why should it be any different with God? He wants to hear our prayers so that He can help us with our problems, to leave more time for us to enjoy Him and His creation. Praise God! If you ask how do we pray? Jesus says how to in Matthew 6:5–15. God says He even intercedes with groaning when we are unable to talk and knows what we need before we ask for it (Romans 8:26, Matthew 6:8). What a great God! Most importantly we need to give our complete will to God and ask that *His will be done in our lives.* As a new creation in Christ we no longer live for ourselves, but for Him (Matthew 6:10).

Now that we have an understanding of how to speak to God, how will we know what His answers are? The best way is to read His Word. Start by asking God about something you have on your mind and then simply open up the Bible to look for an answer. The great thing about God and His Holy Spirit is that He will lead you to the information you need to read. He will speak to you right from the book. This of course takes faith and you have to believe that the Bible is the inspired Word of God and not just written by some men over the last 4,000 years or so (2 Timothy 3:16). However, once you do, you will find a great comfort in knowing that He is and always will be with you (Romans 5:5).

Understanding and reading on your own is a great start, but the only way to fully appreciate and feel the joy, peace and happiness of God is to visit and fellowship with other believers who share your passion and love for our Almighty Creator. As the old saying goes, "Iron sharpens iron" (Proverbs 27:17). In order to find a place that is right for you it may take a while. There are many different ways of worshipping our God. No one is better than the other; however, one may better fit your character and up bringing than another. But never lose sight of the main reason of fellowship and that is to come together and worship our God in unity (1 Corinthians 1:9). Take your time and visit various churches, make sure that they preach salvation in Jesus Christ (2 Timothy 2:10). And lastly, ask God to help find the right one for you!

NOTES

_____

_____

_____

_____

_____

_____

_____

_____

_____

_____

_____

_____

_____

_____

_____

_____

_____

_____

Discussion: Change

"We have learned to turn out lots of goods and services, but we haven't learned as well how to have everybody share in the bounty. The obligation of a society as prosperous as ours is to figure out how nobody gets left to far behind."

—WARREN BUFFET

Business men require a plan in order to succeed at what they want to do. They could be selling any old widget, but if Business Man A is selling the same widget as Business Man B, and Business Man B has a well thought out plan, he is more likely to succeed. When reading and answering questions to this step's discussion make sure that the plans you are developing for your future in Christ are well thought out and led by Him alone!

Discussion Questions

1. No matter what you choose to do in life, whether it is plans to become a billionaire or plans to change the way you live your day to day life, it takes hard work, determination and perseverance. What are a couple of choices you can make or change in your daily routine to start down or better follow the right path?

_____

_____

_____

_____

_____

2. "Right communication" is the key to growth here on earth and above. What types of changes can you make in your communication with others and God in order to "prosper" on your trip down the right path?

_____

_____

_____

_____

_____

3. Giving praise to God is the same as saying thank you! Before moving on with your plans in your new life, write a list of things you have to be thankful for past, present and then into the future!

_____

_____

_____

_____

_____

STEP 4: Restoring Relationships

*"...turn the hearts of the parents to their children
and the disobedient to the wisdom of the righteous—
to make ready a people prepared for the Lord."*

—Luke 1:17

Story: Forgiveness

A boy who had lived his life like most of the other boys in his neighbourhood decided that he wanted to do more with what he had. He had big dreams and they continued to grow larger as he did.

However one day as a young man he realized that there had to be more to life than striving for earthly gain.

He decided to go back to the church of his boyhood and start searching for answers. This decision was the beginning of the dream he was looking for.

Along with the joy of finding likeminded caring people, he also realized he had made many mistakes as a young child and adult that he needed forgiveness for.

This was the start of his path to restoring relationships with the people in his life and God.

Your story might be similar to this one. Take time to read

this chapter and figure out what might be holding you back from accomplishing the dream God has for you!

Lesson: Coming home

Just like restoring our relationship with our Father in heaven, it is important that we take a long look at our past relationships with family, friends, co-workers, coaches, pastors, partners, teachers and the list will go on. How are our relationships or how were they? Do they need some repair? Do some emotional ties need to be let go or angry words need to be forgiven? Not only has Jesus become our advocate to reconnect with our Father in heaven, He has also done the same to restore our relationships on earth with others we may have hurt or others who may have hurt us in the past (2 Corinthians 5:18, 19).

A perfect example is the parable of the prodigal son. Jesus talks of a young man who wants to have his portion of the inheritance while his father is still alive. He is given his share and spends it recklessly in a faraway country on women and partying. He ends up working on a farm for next to no money and comes to the realization that he is being treated no better than the pigs, where he could be back on his dad's farm working for at least a fair wage. He decides to go home and reconcile with his father, who receives him with open arms and a feast. His brother, who stayed home, is jealous at first, but never the less the family is together again (Luke 15:11–32). The point of this story is to let us know that we have all made mistakes and have caused broken relationships, but no matter what, there is always an opportunity to change and make good what was once wrong.

How do we restore those relationships? First, a broken relationship from our past may have taken years or our whole lives to develop. Come to realize it will not take over night to feel like you once did and the relationship may never be the way it once was. The most important thing is that we become clear minded, forgiving and except forgiveness for whatever has happened in the past to us and the other(s) involved (Mark 11:25).

Most broken relationships are a result of a break in *trust* of the other person(s) involved. This could be due to any number of reasons, which are, cheating, abuse, jealousy, lying, hatred and the list goes on. If the other person(s) involved does not have the tools to forgive, you must know that what is most important is that God has forgiven you already. That is the perfect sacrifice Jesus Christ made for us (Romans 5:8). Understand that you will never find the soul fulfilling love from any individual here on earth, like the love from our Father in heaven (Psalm 18:30).

How many times should we forgive? We might say, but this person hurt me so many times, how could I ever forgive them? Jesus says to forgive not seven times, but seventy times seven (Matthew 18:21–35). Or they did a horrible thing that could never be forgiven. Believe it! Jesus Christ died for those sins too! Anything against God is sin no matter how big or small it is to our eyes and mind or society as a whole. God does not treat one person any greater than another (Romans 2:11).

NOTES

_____

_____

_____

_____

_____

_____

_____

_____

_____

_____

_____

_____

_____

_____

_____

_____

_____

_____

Discussion: Mending

"I learned that courage was not the absence of fear, but the triumph over it. The brave man is not he who does not feel afraid, but he who conquers that fear."

—NELSON MANDELA

Politicians are required to do many jobs. They must be business minded, family oriented, diplomatic and self-sacrificing in time and efforts for "the greater good". When reading and answering questions to this step's discussion keep in mind the type of person you want to become and how this affects your relationships with others.

Discussion Questions

1. Nelson Mandela went through many trials in his life, including 27 years in jail, but he persevered to help create independence for his people. Your life's trials may not be as extreme as Mr. Mandela's but never the less you have likely gone through rough times. What is holding you back from taking your next step in life's journey? Write a list of people you need to forgive and write down any words of concern or issues that need to be discussed in each circumstance in order to restore that relationship and move on in your new life.

2. What other steps can you take to mend the relationships and move on in your new life with God and others?

_____

_____

_____

_____

_____

3. What steps can you take to mend your relationship with God if you have been far from him in the past?

_____

_____

_____

_____

STEP 5: Staying On the Path

"Whoever wants to be my disciple must deny themselves
and take up their cross daily and follow me."
—LUKE 9:23

Story: Faith

A woman who was raised during a time of world turmoil and trouble learned to live modestly during times of plenty.

She lived in less than ideal housing conditions as a child and learned to make do with what she had.

As this woman grew older she survived through many other trials with family and friends, but she always stayed on the path God had set for her.

Sometimes staying on the path can be challenging, especially when we have to forgive people from our past and trust that God has full control over the situation, past, present, and future. But once we have submitted ourselves to God's plan it makes helping carry it out much easier. As the Bible says, "take up" your "cross daily" (Luke 9:23).

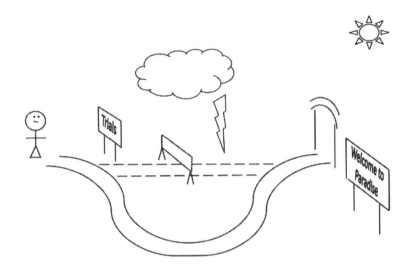

Lesson: Staying True

If you have made it this far, congratulations! Although the subject in this chapter is simple to understand it is crucial in our ability to maintain our new life. We had discussed in Lesson 3 what the right path is, now we will discuss how to stay on it (2 Corinthians 11:3). Most importantly we must fall asleep at night and wake up every day with God on our minds. We must ask ourselves in the morning, what will God have me do today? And pray about it (Jeremiah 10:23). Before we go to bed we must ask God to bring us to rest, ask for forgiveness for whatever we might have done wrong today and thank Him for everything He has given us (Ephesians 4:26).

Remember, whatever happened in our past has been forgiven and it is now time to move on in our new life with Jesus Christ and God the Father. We must put away our old selves and start developing new characteristics, God's characteristics, new habits, new friends and new places of work and commune (Ephesians 4:22). The only way to live this new life is to turn from the old one!

Spending time with God daily is important, not only in prayer, but also in His Word. Pick up the Bible in the morning before you start your day and spend a few minutes grounding yourself in His Word. Do the same thing at night. You will be amazed at how much change comes and how quickly when you are obeying God (Colossians 3:16).

Seek out people who are like minded, who have a thirst and hunger for God like you do. You do not have to spend every day with them, but keep them in your prayers and on your heart (2 Corinthians 6:14).

Lastly, as a new believer, we may start developing idea's that are not biblically sound and take scripture too literal when we study His Word alone. Although every piece of scripture has its purpose we must remember through prayer and speaking with others about God, we will learn much more for ourselves (Proverbs 3:7). And, we must ask questions and prove what is the Truth for ourselves (1 Thessalonians 5:21).

NOTES

_____

_____

_____

_____

_____

_____

_____

_____

_____

Discussion: Strength

"A clear and innocent conscience fears nothing"
—QUEEN ELIZABETH I

Royalty must be an example for the people they reign over. The nation they represent requires of them to be soldier like, business minded, politically involved, but above all they usually have a certain amount of devout faith to their countries common spiritual beliefs. When reading and answering questions to this step's discussion keep in mind the type of relationship you would like to maintain with God in the long term situation here on earth and ever after.

Discussion Questions

1. Queen Elizabeth I was required to be an example for a nation. She may not have been perfect, but she persevered through some of the toughest times of the 20th century. What are some of the right habits we can do on a daily basis to stay on the right path? Write them down.

_____

_____

_____

_____

_____

2. The Bible suggests that a person should pray without ceasing (1 Thessalonians 5:17). What does this mean for you? And develop a list of people, situations and life events you can pray for throughout the day.

_____

_____

_____

_____

_____

3. How can you pray throughout the day without others openly knowing about it?

_____

_____

_____

_____

STEP 6: Helping Others to See

"The Spirit of the Lord is on me, because he has
anointed me to proclaim good news ..."
—LUKE 4:18

Story: Act it out

A husband and wife recently moved to a new neighbourhood with their children and decided to do what they thought was their Chrisitian duty by giving some neighbourly advice to the wayward neighbours. Not realizing it at the time this advice was not taken to kindly and it ended up reflecting back on the couple. After some discussion it was decided that they would act out the Christian life style rather than suggest it to others.

Some times in life it is better just to mind your own business rather than stick your nose in other peoples. The Bible mentions in 1 Thessalonians 4:11, "to lead a quiet life: You should mind your own business and work with your hands..." This would have been grand advice for this couple had they been completely submissive to God and obeying His word. However sometimes in life it is better to go through a trial and learn from it, rather than read about someone else's mistake and learn, as real life experience always stick with a person longer and deeper than fantasy...

Lesson: Giving

At first, the path we have chosen may not seem easy. Deciding to follow Christ takes dedication day after day. Sometimes we slip up, but in the end He is always there for us (2 Corinthians 12:9). We are asked to become images of Christ as we were created physical images from the beginning (Genesis 1:26). But now we must look at our inward man and clean it out, so that we can show others through our change in character who Christ really is (Romans 7:22).

Now more than ever it is important to show Christ's character in us, because a world gone seemingly awry is on a downward spiral to destruction if something does not change and soon (Hebrews 10:25). As men and women of God we must be set apart from the world, there must be a difference in us noticeable enough for someone to ask. What is the hope that is in you (1 Peter 3:15)? And our answer must be Jesus Christ.

God loves a cheerful giver and there are many ways to reach out to others that are in need (2 Corinthians 9:7). We can donate food to the poor, pray for healing of the sick, become friends with someone we may never have cared for in the past, share our testimony and at any time pray for others who are in need (Ephesians 4:28). This is God's way and it is now our way. We have a giving God, look around at everything He has provided for us and know that we must reflect that giving nature in us (Matthew 6:26). Praise the Lord!

A very important area of life where we can show others the Way is our family. Although some of our family members may not be believers, we must still love them just the same (Luke 6:27, 28). We must now become the responsible ones in showing others how to live a just life (Luke 12:48). We must walk the talk (1 Thessalonians 4:11, 12). Even Jesus was responsible for His mother until His death and then entrusted her life over to one of His followers, John (John 19:26, 27).

Most importantly, we must; lead by example, love God, worship Him, and give Him the glory in our lives (Revelation 19:1). And love our neighbours as ourselves (Galatians 5:14).

NOTES

_____

_____

_____

_____

_____

_____

_____

_____

_____

_____

_____

Discussion: Ideas

"Peace cannot be kept by force. It can only
be achieved by understanding."
—ALBERT EINSTEIN

Intellectually gifted people are in a league of their own. Sometimes their ideas are so forward thinking that very few others believe what these individuals are suggesting could come true. These intellects are required to believe in the unseen, much like Christians are to hope in the unseen. When reading and answering the questions to this step's discussions take time to close your eyes and envision plans God may have for you in the future.

Discussion Questions

1. Albert Einstein lived a life of servitude. He dedicated his life to the sciences and helped save the Allied countries from much unnecessary destruction during WWII. How can you walk your Christian walk by doing rather than speaking what you believe is a proper religious perspective? Develop a list of ideas.

_____

_____

_____

_____

_____

2. As Einstein said, understanding is the key to peace. To go further than that read Ecclesiastes 12:12, 13 and reflect on what can be done to help others to see.

_____

_____

_____

_____

_____

3. List some ideas of what you think God is putting on your heart to do in this new life with Christ. Remember no idea too big or too small is unimportant (Zechariah 4:10).

_____

_____

_____

_____

_____

STEP 7: Finishing the Race

"Therefore, since we are surrounded by such a great cloud of witnesses, let us throw off everything that hinders and the sin that so easily entangles. And let us run with perseverance the race marked out for us,"
—Hebrews 12:1

Story: Endurance

A boy who was raised on a farm did not always have an easy life growing up, as he and his family went through difficult times during his childhood. As he was becoming of age the war effort was starting up. He decided he was going to do his part for his country. He left a boy but came back a man.

Upon coming back he settled in his home town and married his high school sweetheart. The two went on to have many beautiful children and grandchildren. He worked for a local car manufacturing company most of his life and did what he could for his community. Yes this man's life was not always easy.

As this man grew older he moved slower, but his wife and children, especially his wife, were always with him. This man did not spend every Sunday at church or preach out loud to his children, wife, or neighbours, but he led the Christian life the best he knew how, with a quiet confidence until the day he died.

As a Christian it is our duty to walk our own Christian walk similar to what this man did. Remember, it is not the material things on earth we can take with us, but the eternal things; love, kindness, peace, joy, goodness, and patience that God cares about (Galatians 5:22).

Lesson: Patience

My friends, this is just the beginning of a glorious and joyful life in Christ Jesus, our Lord and Saviour. Who was, is, and is yet to come (Revelation 1:8). He will never let you down. He will always be there for you when it seems no one else is (Psalm 27:1). You may go through trials and tribulations, however remember that our reward is not here on earth, but up in heaven with God (Matthew 5:12).

In order to run the race we must pace ourselves, patience is the key to our success in Christ Jesus. We did not come to this point in our lives overnight and it will take our whole lives to complete the work God is doing in us (James 1:4). And God only knows what more He will have prepared for us to do in heaven (1 Corinthians 2:9).

In order for Him to reveal more knowledge to us of His plan we must become obedient to Him in all areas of our lives, no matter how difficult it may be to let go of our past. The way to God's heart is by listening to Him (Romans 6:16). He is that still small voice among a world of confusion (1 Kings 19:12).

Finally, our life and liberty are in Jesus Christ. He has set us free from the bondage of our former life (Galatians 5:1). So let us set aside all burdens and sin and run with endurance the race that is set before us, so that on our final day we can say "I have fought the good fight, I have finished the race, I have kept the faith." (2 Timothy 4:7). To God be the Glory!

NOTES

_____

_____

_____

_____

_____

_____

_____

_____

_____

_____

_____

_____

_____

Discussion: Life

*"In the end, it's not the years in your life that
count. It's the life in your years."*

—ABRAHAM LINCOLN

Visionaries, although they may have accomplished some great feat
or led society in some great movement are essentially the same as
the practical man next door, who plants his garden in the spring,
cultivates it throughout the summer and harvests in the fall.
They plant seeds, cultivate them and then watch them grow until
harvest time. When reading and answering the questions to this
step's discussion take time to meditate on and begin nurturing the
seeds that have been planted on your heart, so that during harvest
time your crop will be plenty!

Discussion Questions

1. Overall each of the leaders mentioned throughout the
    discussion sections have had some characteristics in
    common. Perseverance, courage, and a common concern
    for others. Another major trait that leaders require is vision.
    Many visions are mentioned throughout the Bible and
    every leader of this world requires a vision of some sort
    to lead a group of people to a goal. Take some time and
    ask God what your vision might be. Draw it out and start
    writing ideas down on how you may accomplish this vision.

_____

_____

_____

_____

2. In continuing your journey in life and forming your relationships with others and God, what qualities or characteristics would you like to strengthen or remove from your own life in order to develop a better self? List them out and pray about how to develop those qualities you want and get rid of the ones you do not want.

_____

_____

_____

_____

_____

Reader's Guide:
How to use this book

This book was created as a compilation of steps with a short story, Bible study lesson, and discussion questions included in each step in order to provoke thought and opportunity for personal growth in Christ and in a group environment. It is meant for readers of various levels of education so that anyone can have the opportunity to better themselves.

The short stories are used to connect the reader to real life situations of trials and triumphs that take place in our daily lives.

The lesson sections are used to ground the reader in the written word of God in order to lead the reader's daily life with suggestions on how to start or restart one's daily relationships with God and others.

The discussion question sections are used to spark spiritual character development in individual readers and with others in order to help bring the stories and lessons of the Bible to the realities of daily life here on earth. The discussion answers added to some of the questions following are not exhaustive. They are meant for groups and individuals to meditate on and use as they see fit to initiate and develop self-reflection and discussion. The prayer topics are there to help start self-reflection and group prayer as seen fit by those using it.

The main focus of this book is restoring relationships, both with God and others. To this end it is my hope that anyone who takes on a leadership role in sharing the teachings in this book focuses heavily on the magnificent restoring powers of God!

STEP 1: Accepting God's Love— Reader's Guide

Discussion: Knowledge

> *"Where there is love there is life"*
> —MAHATMA GHANDI

Christ laid his life down for us in order to stand for the truth! When reading and answering questions to this step's discussion, focus on the simple things Christ did for us. The discussion answers added to some of the questions below are not exhaustive. They are meant for groups and individuals to meditate on and use as they see fit to initiate and develop self-reflection and discussion.

Discussion Questions

1. How do you relate your personal belief system with other religions, people and belief systems?

Encourage self-reflection and group discussion.

2. Do you look for common ground with yourself and others or do you separate yourself from others based on differences?

Encourage self-reflection and group discussion. Read Exodus 22:21, Ephesians 6:5 – 9

Alienation can take place very easily in this world. We are told numerous times in the Bible to take care of our slaves, and those foreigners who live in our country. As a society we must look past colour and culture and take a look at the deep rooted commonalities we all have; hunger and thirst, a desire for knowledge and better quality of life, care and concern for elders and children, etc.

These common needs and desires should bring people of different cultures and skin colour together under any nation's flag!

3. How can a person reconcile ones' belief system with other religions, people and belief systems? List some ideas.

Encourage self-reflection and group discussion. Readers can look to the Golden Rule for a start.

4. How do you relate your faith journey with respect to the roots of Christianity? That is, the people (Jesus, Paul, Peter, etc.) previously of the Jewish faith whom it was founded by.

Encourage self-reflection and group discussion. Read John 4:22 and Romans 3:1, 2 "Salvation is from the Jews".

Mainstream Christianity celebrates the Sabbath on Sunday. However some Christian groups and Judaism celebrate the Sabbath on Saturday. The military has a saying "a C is a P and the weekends are free", meaning in training a "C" grade is a pass and you have the weekends off! Western governments have a similar philosophy with closing up offices during the weekend.

The Christian realm might do well to integrate these government philosophies so as to not step on each other's toes when it comes to arguing about specific doctrines. Above putting a certain day aside for rest, let us "rejoice in the Lord always" (Philippians 4:4)!

5. **Pick out at least one place in the New Testament that suggests Jesus was a practicing Jew.**

Encourage self-reflection and group discussion. Read John 7 to start.

Prayer: Topic Suggestions

- Love
- Sacrifice
- Forgiveness
- Elderly, fatherless, widows and poor
- Unity in diversity

STEP 2: What Should We Do?— Reader's Guide

Discussion: Planning

> *"The destiny of man is not measured by material computation, when great forces are on the move in the world, we learn we are spirits, not animals."*
> —SIR WINSTON CHURCHILL

Soldiers of our nations are expected to make the ultimate sacrifice for their country and fellow man when asked to. Never are they asked to blindly lose their lives. They are part of a calculated and accurately made "bigger plan". When reading and answering questions to this step's discussion keep in mind what purpose God has for you in His "bigger plan". The discussion answers added to some of the questions below are not exhaustive. They are meant for groups and individuals to meditate on and use as they see fit to initiate and develop self-reflection and discussion.

Discussion Questions

1. *What choices do you have to make in your life currently? List them out and make clear the options you can take for each of them.*

Encourage self-reflection and group discussion. Examples may include, looking for a new job, buying a new home, buying a new car, changing various personal relationship situations, accepting Christ as ruler of our life, etc.

2. *If it came down to it would you be ready to make the ultimate sacrifice for your beliefs? Why or why not?*

Encourage self-reflection and group discussion.

3. *What changes can you make in your daily routine that will have a positive impact on you and the world around you?*

Encourage self-reflection and group discussion. Examples may include, reading the Bible or praying more often, etc.

4. *What choices have you made in the past that have changed your life, positive or negative? List them out.*

Encourage self-reflection and group discussion.

5. *If negative, what can you do to use those negative choices and turn them into positives for yourself and others who can learn from them?*

Encourage self-reflection and group discussion. An example would be over drinking often, which negatively affects performance levels in completing daily tasks. The positive would be stopping the negative habit and talking to others who have the same problem, encouraging them that they too can free themselves of the overindulging habit.

Prayer: Topic Suggestions

- Acceptance
- Government/Authority
- Military Service Members
- Discernment
- Decisions

STEP 3: The Right Path— Reader's Guide

Discussion: Change

> *"We have learned to turn out lots of goods and services, but we haven't learned as well how to have everybody share in the bounty. The obligation of a society as prosperous as ours is to figure out how nobody gets left to far behind."*
> —WARREN BUFFET

Business men require a plan in order to succeed at what they want to do. They could be selling any old widget, but if Business Man A is selling the same widget as Business Man B, and Business Man B has a well thought out plan, he is more likely to succeed. When reading and answering questions to this step's discussion make sure that the plans you are developing for your future in Christ are well thought out and led by Him alone! The discussion answers added to some of the questions below are not exhaustive. They are meant for groups and individuals to meditate on and use as they see fit to initiate and develop self-reflection and discussion.

Discussion Questions

1. *No matter what you choose to do in life, whether it is plans to become a billionaire or plans to change the way you live your day to day life, it takes hard work, determination and perseverance. What are a couple of choices you can make or change in your daily routine to start down or better follow the right path?*

Encourage self-reflection and group discussion. In regards to the Bible study lesson you should, Pray, Read the Bible, Fellowship and Worship God. However this is not an exhaustive list of changes especially for anyone who has developed "bad habits" throughout life. Other changes may include, drinking less alcohol, acting more mercifully, spending more time with loved ones, etc.

2. *"Right communication" is the key to growth here on earth and above. What types of changes can you make in your communication with others and God in order to "prosper" on your trip down the right path?*

Encourage self-reflection and group discussion.

3. *Giving praise to God is the same as saying thank you! Before moving on with your plans in your new life, write a list of things you have to be thankful for past, present and then into the future!*

Encourage self-reflection and group discussion. And don't just be thankful for the good things. Read 1 Thessalonians 5:18 and Philippians 4 for more insight.

Prayer: Topic Suggestions

- Community Prosperity
- Direction
- Thankfulness
- Wisdom
- Patience

STEP 4: Restoring Relationships— Reader's Guide

Discussion: Mending

"I learned that courage was not the absence of fear, but the triumph over it. The brave man is not he who does not feel afraid, but he who conquers that fear."
—NELSON MANDELA

Politicians are required to do many jobs. They must be business minded, family oriented, diplomatic and self-sacrificing in time and efforts for "the greater good". When reading and answering questions to this step's discussion keep in mind the type of person you want to become and how this affects your relationships with others. The discussion answers added to some of the questions below are not exhaustive. They are meant for groups and individuals to meditate on and use as they see fit to initiate and develop self-reflection and discussion.

Discussion Questions

1. *Nelson Mandela went through many trials in his life, including 27 years in jail, but he persevered to help create independence for his people. Your life's trials may not be as extreme as Mr. Mandela's but never the less you have likely gone through rough times. What is holding you back from taking your next step in life's journey? Write a list of people you need to forgive and write down any words of concern or issues that need to be discussed in each circumstance in order to restore that relationship and move on in your new life.*

Encourage self-reflection and group discussion. As in the study the list may include, teachers, co-workers, friends, family, partners, etc. Exhaust the list in order to bring to light the people and issues involved.

Remember these issues did not crop up overnight. Take time to confront each concern and person.

You may find in some circumstances the other party involved never thought about the issue. However what is most important is that YOU are moving on in your new life with Christ.

2. *What other steps can you take to mend the relationships and move on in your new life with God and others?*

Encourage self-reflection and group discussion. Read Matthew 18

3. *What steps can you take to mend your relationship with God if you have been far from him in the past?*

Encourage self-reflection and group discussion. Pray, Read God's Word, Praise God and Fellowship. Review Step 3 Lesson for more. And remember that each person is at a different stage in their journey with God, so be patient.

Prayer: Topic Suggestions

- Family
- Friends
- Coworkers
- Reconciliation
- Patience

STEP 5: Staying On the Path— Reader's Guide

Discussion: Strength

"A clear and innocent conscience fears nothing"
—QUEEN ELIZABETH I

Royalty must be an example for the people they reign over. The nation they represent requires of them to be soldier like, business minded, politically involved, but above all they usually have a certain amount of devout faith to their countries common spiritual beliefs. When reading and answering questions to this step's discussion keep in mind the type of relationship you would like to maintain with God in the long term situation here on earth and ever after. The discussion answers added to some of the questions below are not exhaustive. They are meant for groups and individuals to meditate on and use as they see fit to initiate and develop self-reflection and discussion.

Discussion Questions

1. *Queen Elizabeth I was required to be an example for a nation. She may not have been perfect, but she persevered through some of the toughest times of the 20th century. What are some of the right habits we can do on a daily basis to stay on the right path? Write them down.*

Encourage self-reflection and group discussion. Review Step 3: Question 1, and revamp your answers as needed, for a renewed look at how you would like to spend your daily life here on earth with others and in a continually strengthened relationship with God. Again, every life in a relationship with God should be grounded in His Word, prayer, fellowship and worship daily.

2. *The Bible suggests that a person should pray without ceasing (1 Thessalonians 5:17). What does this mean for you? Develop a list of people, situations and life events you can pray for throughout your day.*

Encourage self-reflection and group discussion. Ceasing means "to stop", so without ceasing means without stopping. We are encouraged by the words of the Bible to never stop praying, morning, afternoon and night, in shopping lines, out for dinner at a restaurant, and at work. We should be continually praying for the people around us, life events and for the situations we walk into, etc.

Also keep in mind that praying is like having a conversation with another person. God does not need you to be detailed and "wordy". All he wants to hear is what is on your mind, because he already knows (Matthew 9:4). The simplest prayer to do is "Your will be done God". Sometimes we have other types of conversations with God that are more heartfelt and involve tears, but that is where the closet comes in to play (Matthew 6:6). Remember, prayer is like talking with other humans, often it is very gentle and simple requests, but there are times of frustration, disappointment, defeat and severe repentance that is required.

3. How can you pray throughout the day without others openly knowing about it?

Encourage self-reflection and group discussion. Keep in mind, it's possible to pray with your eyes open and mouth closed, but it takes some practice.

Prayer: Topic Suggestions

- Mercy
- Respect
- Loyalty
- Courage
- Endurance

STEP 6: Helping Others to See— Reader's Guide

Discussion: Ideas

> *"Peace cannot be kept by force. It can only be achieved by understanding."*
> —ALBERT EINSTEIN

Intellectually gifted people are in a league of their own. Sometimes their ideas are so forward thinking that very few others believe what these individuals are suggesting could come true. These intellects are required to believe in the unseen, much like Christians are to hope in the unseen. When reading and answering the questions to this step's discussions take time to close your eyes and envision plans God may have for you in the future. The discussion answers added to some of the questions below are not exhaustive. They are meant for groups and individuals to meditate on and use as they see fit to initiate and develop self-reflection and discussion.

Discussion Questions

1. *Albert Einstein lived a life of servitude. He dedicated his life to the sciences and helped save the Allied countries from much unnecessary destruction during WWII. How can you walk your Christian walk by doing rather than speaking what you believe is a proper religious perspective? Develop a list of ideas you believe God is putting on your heart to do in order to show others who Christ is.*

Encourage self-reflection and group discussion. To get started suggestions made in the Bible study are: pray for others, feed the poor, talk to others you may never have before. Remember, leading by example is the best way to show others who Christ really is. As the Bible says, "work out your salvation with fear and trembling" (Philippians 2:12).

2. *As Einstein said, understanding is the key to peace. To go further than that read Ecclesiastes 12:12, 13 and reflect on what can be done to help others to see.*

Encourage self-reflection and group discussion. As Ecclesiastes 12:12, 13 suggests fear God and listen to Him.

3. *List some ideas of what you think God is putting on your heart to do in this new life with Christ. Remember no idea too big or too small is unimportant (Zechariah 4:10).*

Encourage self-reflection and group discussion. Some ideas are finding a new job, picking up an old hobby, sharing more time with family, etc.

Prayer: Topic Suggestions

- Understanding
- Acceptance
- Patience
- Perseverance
- Fellowship

STEP 7: Finishing the Race— Reader's Guide

Discussion: Life

> *"In the end, it's not the years in your life that count. It's the life in your years."*
> —ABRAHAM LINCOLN

Visionaries, although they may have accomplished some great feat or led society in some great movement are essentially the same as the practical man next door, who plants his garden in the spring, cultivates it throughout the summer and harvests in the fall. They plant seeds, cultivate them and then watch them grow until harvest time. When reading and answering the questions to this step's discussion take time to meditate on and begin nurturing the seeds that have been planted on your heart, so that during harvest time your crop will be plenty! The discussion answers added to some of the questions below are not exhaustive. They are meant for groups and individuals to meditate on and use as they see fit to initiate and develop self-reflection and discussion.

Discussion Questions

1. *Overall each of the leaders mentioned throughout the discussion sections have had some characteristics in common. Perseverance, courage, and a common concern for others. Another major trait that leaders require is vision. Many visions are mentioned throughout the Bible and every leader of this world requires a vision of some sort to lead a group of people to a goal. Take some time and ask God what your vision might be. Draw it out and start writing ideas down on how you may accomplish this vision.*

Encourage self-reflection and group discussion. The vision that is developing in your mind may be as simple as starting to learn a new language or as big as starting your own business. Nurture your vision and in time it will develop to what you want it to be. Remember every great accomplishment in this world started with an idea, a seed, a VISION! As President Lincoln said "It's the LIFE in your years" that are important.

2. *In continuing your journey in life and forming your relationships with others and God, what qualities or characteristics would you like to strengthen or remove from your own life in order to develop a better self? List them out and pray about how to develop those qualities you want and get rid of the ones you do not want.*

Encourage self-reflection and group discussion. The key to growth in Christ is getting rid of the old person. It is a lifelong practice and unfortunately you may maintain some of the scars from your past for your entire life. However those scars need not be burdens, but only reminders of your temporal body and what it has been through to prepare yourself for a much greater purpose for eternity! When developing your list, think seriously about the person you want to become in the long-term. Character traits such as honesty, loyalty, patience, joyfulness, courage and strength through Christ are qualities you might want to consider in your journey to your happily ever after!

Prayer: Topic Suggestions

- Endurance
- Provisions
- Opportunities
- Charity
- Servitude

NOTES

NOTES

NOTES

NOTES